One Week in May

on the Beautiful Isles of Scilly

by

Cathy Mayes

Independently Published by Cathy Mayes

First Published 2022 Cathy Mayes

Copyright © 2022, Cathy Mayes

Contact:
Cathyfreelance15@outlook.com
Facebook: Cathy Mayes Author
Instagram: cathy_author

ISBN: 9798847831680

Introduction

Over a few visits I have built up an affinity with the Isles of Scilly, a place so often talked about and described as being tropical, beautiful and interesting; all of which is true. So many happy memories. The long white sandy beaches could just as easily be on the Indian Ocean, and the plants are similar to those that I have seen in South Africa, and other countries. The islands have a microclimate that supports many plant species, migrating birds, including the American goshawk and the blue-cheeked bee-eater, from Eastern Europe; white sands sprinkled with glitter, every blue, lilac, purple and green you can imagine in the colours of the sea, and to add to the array, and memorable sea of colour, there are the bright coloured boats bobbing up and down on their moorings, transporting people from island to island, and island to school, along with the post, and fishing boats. All the colours of the rainbow can be seen on the Isles of Scilly, even without the rain!

This was to be my fifth visit to the Isles. My first time was in 1979 with my first husband Tony, we were celebrating our third wedding anniversary, we had our daughter Elaine with us, just six months old. We sailed on a very rough day in October, Tony was not a keen sailor, so we stayed inside, and I tried to stop him watching the undulating sea through the porthole, as it made it look far worse than it was. We stayed at Pelistry Bay, diagonally across the island from Hugh Town on the main Island of St Mary's. We realised quite quickly that the pushchair was not the best mode of transport for walking around the cliff paths to the town and exploring the Garrison. We used the baby carrier and whilst we had some damp weather, we also had beautiful autumn days of sunshine, the light was stunning. Our bed and breakfast were comfortable, our hosts welcoming, and could not have been more helpful in catering for us all.

My second visit was with a dear friend, Mary. She loved the islands and visited almost every year, inviting various friends to accompany her on her trip. It was September 2005 and I had four days annual leave to use, so I stayed with Mary in a little bed and breakfast at Porth Mellon. We walked our way around the island, and took several boat trips, one to Tresco, where we spent the day looking around the amazing Old Abbey gardens. The gardens are tropical, beautiful, varied, with so many aspects to explore, as well as features such as sculptures and figureheads from ships of long ago, in the Valhalla Museum.

My parents inherited a figurehead when they bought our house. It had come from the Viola, the ship had been built at Appledore shipyard in 1872 and had several owners before being bought by Captain John Henry Male Master Mariner of St Minver 30th April 1884, he then sold her to John Male farmer at St Minver 3rd July 1884, perhaps his brother, cousin, or uncle. Subsequently on 6th December 1889 the Viola was sold back to Captain John Henry Male.

John Male died 20th September 1905, John Henry was the executor of the estate and sold the Viola on to William Hitchings ship owner of Middle Street Padstow. She had several more owners before she went aground on the rocks at Kennick near the Lizard, in fog, she was carrying China Clay from Teignmouth to Glasgow. Whilst it was said that she was taken to Falmouth and broken up, an advertisement did appear in the Western Morning News announcing the auction of Viola September 19th 1922, she was fifty years old, I assume that was a reasonable age for a schooner that had dodged the major action in the war, despite having been set up as a Q boat.

Q boats were 'to be decoy vessels, special service ships, or mystery ships, were heavily armed merchant ships with concealed weaponry, designed to *lure submarines into making surface attacks. This gave Q-ships the chance to open fire and sink them'.* (**en.wikipedia.org/wiki/Q-ship**)

What was particularly interesting for me was when I visited the museum on Tresco I saw another figurehead fashioned in a similar style to the one my family owns. I began to wonder if there had been a sister ship, for the figureheads to be so alike. I contacted the Appledore museum, they sent me photographs of Viola, it was wonderful to see her, though sadly not displaying the figurehead. It is likely that these photos were taken after she was commissioned as a Q boat and the figurehead had been removed. Most of the information I have included about the Viola came from the museum, they have been so helpful; and guess what, the museum tells me

'The Viola was one of two schooners built for Earle, Earle and Haller. The other was called Silvia and she too ended up in a Cornish port, this time Fowey. She also had a third mast fitted (in 1895) and was sunk by a submarine in WWI.'

So perhaps the Silvia's figurehead ended up in the museum on Tresco. I was so thrilled to have this history to add to what we already knew about Viola; she has been in our lives since my parents bought the house back in the 50s. Even more exciting is to have the photographs of her. Whilst owning Viola, John Male, master, also owned the Lizzie Male, a Padstow built schooner, there is a painting of her dated February 17th, 1873. So much history and wonderful people who are happy to share what they know. I had wondered if the figurehead of Viola came back to Captain JH Male as a gift after she had been broken up, or whether he brought it from the salvage. Now I suspect that it had been removed several years prior to her fate.

During our few days Mary and I took a trip out to the Eastern Isles to see the seals, the sea was choppy, and good fun, we were rather wet by the time we returned to dry land. Mary stood with the boatman the whole journey and it turned out that he was a distant cousin. We walked around St Mary's, visited the lovely café at St Juliet's Gardens and walked up to Telegraph Hill. Old Quay offered a tiny café for a welcome drink and snack having walked around Peninnis Head by the lighthouse. We visited St Martin's and joined in the rowdy singing at the hotel, where the gig rowers and their followers had descended for the afternoon.

Typically, by the time I had to leave, to return home and to work, the sun came out and the weather was beautiful and very warm for September. Mary opted to stay for a few more days to bask in the sun, having changed her Scillonian ticket for a flight; she had not enjoyed the choppy seas on the way over! We had revelled in cool, mostly sunny days and I felt quite relaxed on my sail home, leaving Mary behind to find out more about her Isles of Scilly relatives and to enjoy some lazy days in the sun.

My third visit 2013, October once again, and it poured with rain for most of our visit. Ian, my husband and I stayed on St Mary's which, given the weather was a good choice as there are several places to visit such as the Star Castle, now a hotel, originally built in 1593 on Garrison Hill to defend the Islands. The museum, whilst small was packed with fascinating items and information, giving a wonderful overview of the history of The Isles of Scilly, the archaeology, geology, and also family history, for those interested in genealogy.

We visited St Juliet's Garden once again, where we had tea with the sparrows enjoying every crumb available to them, whilst sitting happily and patiently around the rim of our plates. Of course, it did not rain all the time, and we enjoyed many walks around the island, seeing the Cairns, the beautiful wind-blown trees and the sea in all directions, though more greys than blues.

We walked to Old Town and visited the churchyard there, which was interesting and linked well with our visit to the museum. The graves put the stories of the island wrecks into perspective and gave a history of its own. One of the ships that floundered on the Rettarier Ledges was the SS Schiller one of the largest ships of her day, launched 1873. She was a German ship making her way from New York via Plymouth to Hamberg. One of the obelisks in the graveyard is dedicated to Louise Holzmaister who drowned that day along with 300 others, 7th May 1875. Louise's husband had the obelisk constructed in her memory. We saw many other graves for people from that same wreck **https://cornwallyesteryear.com** The SS Schillers wreck was the largest loss of life since 1707 which had involved four Royal Naval vessels including the HMS Association, Eagle, Romney and Firebrand all returning home together from the Mediterranean. This occurred because of their inability to accurately determine their longitude and caused a loss of approximately 2000 people **https://en.wikipedia.org/**

Harold Wilson, former Prime Minister, who loved the Isles of Scilly and had a house there is also buried in this graveyard.

Our accommodation backed on to the Garrison walls and we could see the canons from the sitting room. In the other direction we had an amazing view of the sea, the boats, Buzza Hill, Porthcressa and Town Beach. We had several steps to climb up to our apartment and it was well worth it, to have such a stunning view. Mary had hoped to join us on this trip, though sadly she was not well enough when the time came, and actually we would have had difficulty getting her up and down the steps, she was not one to have been satisfied just looking at the view!

With self-catering, we had plenty of space to hang, and dry our wet clothes. We found a great café serving fresh caught fish, and on other occasions we cooked for ourselves. I remember it being a rather bumpy sail home on this occasion, and extremely wet for most of the journey though we still opted for being on deck with so much to see. The waves were crashing high above Long Rock presenting quite a picture, though not one that could be captured on camera, well not by me! However, the light was amazing as we came into Penzance harbour, the welcome, a picture of masts and boats to the left, and the beautiful mystic St Michael's Mount to our right with the sun just going down with mellow mauves and yellows.

When my friend Rosy invited me to join her and her daughter for a week, my first time to stay on St Martin's; and return to the beautiful Isles in 2017, I was very quick to accept. It was also my first time of bringing my dog with me, Bertie was still a puppy really, well two years old, I think he always will behave like a pup, he has far too much energy to be anything else! A cocker-cross with springer-spaniel; who certainly has the spring! Bertie is the most loyal, adorable dog, he is clever, and adores cuddles and treats!

We had such a wonderful time, the two dogs, Bertie and Rosy's Misty, thoroughly enjoyed themselves. Rosy and I found some beautiful walks, along with plenty of relaxation. Bertie can be a little exuberant and I remember one morning, we had been for a long walk and ended up on the part of beach between Lawrence's Bay and Par Beach. The rocks and boulders were huge, and we found one shaped like an armchair, it was a climb to get up to it. Bertie and Misty were running about, in and out of the water and as usual Bertie amused himself digging in the sand. Rosy and I were quite comfortable enjoying the sun and looking out to sea, when I was pounced on by an extremely wet and sandy dog. Bertie is not a small dog and he gave me quite a fright, I did not see him coming as he jumped from the side, landing right in my lap! All I could hear was people laughing, Rosy joined in, once her mouth closed from the shock. The laughter was coming from a young couple stretched out on the cliff overlooking the beach. They must have seen it coming!

Bertie has not done this before, though he does love plenty of attention and cuddles, particularly in the evening. Thankfully with the sun shining I dried out fairly quickly as we continued our walk, our peace and tranquillity only temporarily interrupted. He clearly thought it was time to move on!

Rosy invited Bertie and me to accompany her again the following year, for one week in May, how exciting!

One Week in May

A week on the beautiful Isles of Scilly. Twenty-eight miles SW of Cornwall, lie these magical archipelagos with blue, green and mauve spangled seas, lapping onto white sands glinting with sparkling mica.

Bertie, my springer cross cocker spaniel and I sail off on The Scillonian, with Rosy and her border collie Misty.

Day 1, May 2018

The evening before sailing, I drove down to Rosy's cottage, about an hour and a half from where I live; taking my case and all of Bertie's paraphernalia, food, bed, rug to absorb water, dishes, lead, balls and thrower etc. We stayed overnight at Rosy's, in her beautiful cottage tucked into the valley, not too far from Penzance.

We rose early, to a chilly, grey morning. The car was packed the night before, we added the last-minute items, such as dogs and their food. Bertie and Misty, had been out in the garden to play and stretch their legs. This was Bertie's second voyage on the Scillonian, the ship that would take us the twenty-eight miles across to the main Island of St Mary's. At 7.15am we put the dogs in the car and off we set, kindly driven to the Isles of Scilly Steam Ship which would be docked and waiting in Penzance; by Rosy's partner. On the way we stopped off to give the dogs a good run near the sea. They were about to have a three-hour journey on the boat and so we needed them to be tired, and also try to avoid any embarrassing little accidents. Having dropped us off with our baggage, food supplies and the dogs; Rosy's partner then took himself off to the airport, he prefers to fly and perhaps to have some peace from us, and our dogs!

Baggage checked in, boarding passes in one hand and dogs on leads in the other, we walked up the gang plank. Whilst we had waited in the queue, a staff member had walked along announcing that there was 'no way to soften the pill, it was to be a rough crossing!' She advised anyone who might need it to take something for sea sickness as soon as they boarded the ship. Even before we hauled ropes and weighed anchor for our journey, people were turning green!

Having boarded the Scillonian, we headed to the stern and found our favourite place, sheltered behind the bulkhead. If it was to be a wet and rocky ride, we needed somewhere sheltered and plenty of fresh air, a cure for everything in my book! By the time we steamed out of the harbour there were less than a dozen people sitting up front and outside. Several people had been soaked by the spray splashing off the harbour walls and decided to go inside. During the forty-five minutes that we had to wait to set sail, the dogs took time to settle, eventually snuggling as close as they could to us or under the seats to keep dry from the rain. Rosy and I had full waterproofs and layers of warm clothing, a must for this journey as we have learned over the years.

Great excitement, we know that we are set to have an amazing week, no matter what the weather. The dogs love the freedom on the islands and where we are staying on St Martin's there are so many beautiful spaces. As we left the harbour, the boat had to turn around, we had a good 'rock and roll' as the waves hit broadside. Once we were underway and sailing against the wind we settled into the rise and fall of the sea. It was a gloomy morning and whilst we could see the coast disappearing, it was partly enveloped by cloud and drizzle. There would be little chance of seeing dolphins today, or the Minack theatre set into the cliffs above Porthcurno beach, or other vessels, tankers and fishing boats, and no chance at all of seeing Rosy's partner flying overhead, for his fifteen-minute journey to the Islands.

As we advanced passed Long Rock, hidden, shrouded in misty rain, the waves became bigger. Rosy fixed her gaze on the horizon, we had eaten as soon as we boarded the boat, toasted sandwich for Rosy, porridge for me along with coffee and tea respectively. Rosy had also brought gingerbread with her as it is good for settling the stomach on these sorts of occasions; a wonderful tonic for sailing the high seas. Lucky for me I am quite happy with rough seas, so just enjoyed the gingerbread anyway!

The dogs were so good, Misty hunkered down under Rosy's seat, Bertie preferred to sit beside me, or on my lap, to get the maximum attention from both me and other passengers. The drizzle became more persistent as we sailed towards St Mary's, the largest island of the archipelago; we experienced crashing waves and on several occasions the bow rose to about forty-five degrees, the stern followed in its wake, then came the thud of the wave hitting the hull.

The rain was collecting and swimming around the deck, the bottom of our bags drenched, so pleased that my notebook, pen and book were in a sealed plastic bag. The dogs were bedraggled, soggy, cold and doll-eyed. Bertie shivering from cold and perhaps a little bit of excitement. I rubbed him all over to keep the circulation going and dried him as much as possible, I had a super absorbent towel with me, though he absolutely hates being towel-dried. Misty came out from under the seat, took a look around her, checked that Rosy was still there and hid back under the seat, looking queasy, if that is possible for a dog.

Once we saw the coastline of St Martin's we knew we did not have far to go. We needed to stand up to find our legs, it had not been safe to move around the boat as we would usually have done. We had seen other passengers try and they had struggled to stay upright. One fellow was tossed across the deck into the railings and was visibly shocked by the experience, poor soul.

The boat docked and we began to disembark. At the same time the crane was hauling the baggage containers of luggage and provisions over the harbour wall and off the ship. Rosy's partner met us at the harbour, and guess what, he was looking, relaxed, fresh and very dry!

Bertie was so pleased to be moving again that he just flew down the gangway and I had to let go of his extending lead or I would have been flat on my face. The boatman kindly grabbed the lead and held him for me. I doubt he would have gone very far; it was just his usual energy and perhaps a need to be on dry, stable land. The rain was absolutely pelting down like stair rods, and all of us passengers congregated along the harbour, under cover where we could. We were already so wet, it really made no difference at that stage, though we still tried to seek shelter. Baggage was unloaded straight onto the inter-island boats and then once loaded they came alongside the harbour wall for us to board, according to which island we were staying on. A wonderful service, your luggage already loaded for you and you are taken over to your island to begin your holiday. The Isles of Scilly are all about the sea, the island transport, boats and tides. Bertie decided that with such a busy boat the best place to sit was on my lap. I have never known the boat so busy, there literally was no space unused and with several dogs on board and luggage, it was difficult climbing over people to get to the few spaces that we were being shown us by the boatman. Twenty minutes and the dogs could run on the beautiful (even in the rain) beach on St Martin's and we could relax. The weather was at last improving and the sky was lighter with a hint of sunshine behind the clouds. We had enjoyed an exciting and adventurous crossing from Penzance to St Mary's and then the small boat to St. Martin's, at least I had, I cannot speak for Rosy. Our host was at Higher Town Quay waiting to meet us and to collect our luggage, taking us up to the lovely granite cottage of North Farm, where we have stayed for a couple of years now. Rosy walked up with the dogs so that they could stretch and run for a while. I had a lift with the luggage, and was grateful for that.

Once we had unloaded, made ourselves comfortable and eaten a very late lunch, Rosy and I took the dogs for a well-earned walk. A very short time on the leads and they were off. St Martin's is a dog paradise, one lane, more than road through the island, hardly any cars, tracks and paths everywhere to run and enjoy, the dogs I mean, I don't run! We are surrounded by the sea and clifftops covered in yellow gorse and purple heather along with untold species of wildflowers and beautiful grasses.

We walked down to Lawrence's Bay, close to where the school is, dogs darting through marram grasses and down to the water's edge. We threw the balls for them and they happily retrieved and returned for more. Bertie has a liking for seaweed and spent some time, tearing up clumps of it, already detached from its source, it must be the salt that he likes. He buried his ball under the weed, found it, buried it again, great game, so easily pleased. Despite having been soaked to the skin once today, Bertie plunged into the water, he loves swimming, catching the ball in the water and generally rushing about. Quite exhausting to watch. Whilst he swam amongst some weed, a large, long piece of bladder wrack attached itself to his tail, his ever-present propeller. He took little notice and continued to bound about with this extension for some time before it dislodged. He watched the receding waves take his ball and then pounced on it as if it were alive.

Having played with the dogs, sat on the rocks and lifted our faces to the sun that had deigned to come out from behind the cloud, we decided it was time to head back to the cottage. As we walked along the beach, I found what appeared to be a short cut through the dunes. It took us a great deal of effort and hilarity to get to the top. For every step we took, we slipped back three. We were bent double with laughing, exhausted, and the dogs just looked down at us as if to say, just what do you think you are doing there.

Finally, we reached the cottage. After we had supper, a read in front of the open fire; an early night was a relief to us all after a busy, exhausting, adventurous start to our holiday.

Day 2

Woke up to a glorious blue sky and some warmth in the air despite the early hour. I had heard Rosy go down to make her early coffee and also heard the back door open, so I knew she had let the dogs out into the garden. I turned over and dozed for a little longer. The dogs started making quite a hullabaloo as they rushed around on the lovely wooden floor-boards downstairs which echoed through the cottage. Bertie not being used to stairs, made a few mad rushes up and down, though I had to tell him to go down, as dogs are not allowed upstairs, a system I totally agree with. He does tend to have a mad five minutes every now and then. If only I had his energy!

Eventually I dragged myself out of the very comfortable bed and went downstairs to get a cup of tea, whilst the kettle boiled, took the dogs back out to the garden for another run. Rosy must have nipped back to bed. Whilst the dogs did calm down, they were clearly wanting to be out and about again. An hour later they were keen to be off on their first walk of the day. I am sure they knew they were on holiday and remembered the regime from last year. After all, that is what we are here for, to enjoy this amazing island, to perhaps visit some of the others, to walk, relax, watch and listen to the birds whilst taking in the delights of cliff paths and wildflowers. And of course, to give our undivided attention to our beautiful bouncy, canine friends.

We had a quick breakfast ourselves, having fed the dogs. We then left and went for our first walk of the day. It is a joy to be able to walk out the door and not to have to take the dogs anywhere in a car to start their walk. At home we both live in beautiful areas of Cornwall, though to take the dogs walking without leads, it is necessary to drive somewhere first, albeit in my case only about five minutes. Somehow, just walking out of the door and along a lane where there is virtually no traffic is perfect dog country.

We left the cottage taking the lane to the left, the sea, St Mary's and the Eastern Isles were on our right towards St Martin's Head. The sun was shining, the sea a deep and vivid blue, with ripples of purple and turquoise glimmering through the surface. We followed the path towards Bread and Cheese Cove, a beautiful horseshoe shaped bay with a white sandy beach offering a deep channel for shelter, I cannot find where its name originated except that perhaps, because of the safety it offers and the beauty of the area, it is a great place to moor your boat and eat. The Daymark, painted in thick stripes of red and white, originally white limewashed all over, can be seen by ships in the light of day and the darkest of nights, it is to our right. It was apparently built in 1683 by Thomas Ekins to help the sailors navigate this difficult coast and to perhaps to lead them to the shelter of Bread and Cheese Cove. Was the name of the cove linked to the rock formation perhaps?

We are crossing the section of the island from one coast to the other over Chapel Down. At the highest point of our walk, we had a bird's eye view of the whole island. The scenery stunning and variance of light, amazing. On one side we had grey sky and slate-coloured seas, on the other, silver sea reflecting the sun and on the third, bright blue sea and sky. So completely different, and yet surrounding one small island. If I had not seen it, I may not have believed it could appear so unconnected.

Having checked out the landmarks, we found a lane and a field which brought us through to Churchtown Farm where they send their beautiful flowers to many lucky customers. We passed the Coastguard and Fire Station. To our left was a little church, Church of England, built in 1866, it had a single stained-glass window and a gallery accessed from a wooden staircase. The graveyard was spotless and even the most ancient of gravestones were receiving the best of care. We wondered back to the cottage having bought a few postcards from the one and only shop, which incidentally sells everything you might need. Food and dairy products can be ordered and are brought over from the mainland, it is a well-stocked shop.

We had a couple of hours, reading and relaxing in the garden, after a snack lunch whilst the sun shared its warmth. I took a stroll to the shop and posted my cards and then went to visit the art gallery for a browse. There were several people there, including a travel writer. A local artist is working with the school children this week, I am looking forward to seeing their work. When I returned to the cottage, I made some notes whilst the dogs dozed in the sun by my feet.

In the evening Rosy and I walked again to Lawrence Bay, the dogs had a wonderful time, digging, chewing seaweed, swimming and catching the ball. It is fun to throw the ball at the blackened rocks and watch the dogs as it ricochets off in unexpected directions; this seems to add to Bertie's enjoyment of finding the ball which he does by 'quartering' the area as gun dogs do. There was a cruise ship anchored off St Mary's, the passengers will have had a day visiting St Mary's Island, enjoying the wide choice of eateries and shops; perhaps they will have walked up to Juliet's Garden and enjoyed the stunning views as they sip their tea, perhaps indulging in a cream tea, jam first of course! I seem to remember that several cruise ships visit the island over the summer months, and I assume that the island enjoys a boost in revenue with so many visitors. I am not sure whether there is enough time for the people to visit any of the other islands, though I suspect that some may take a trip on the small boats and do the round trip to the Eastern Isles watching the seals.

In complete contrast to the large cruise ship, a group of people kayaking, paddled passed heading towards Bryer, such a relaxing scene. The sun still had strength and the sky was blue, the sea glinting silver beneath bursts of cloud floating gently above the sea. We collected driftwood so that we could have a small fire in the cottage again tonight. The evenings are still quite chilly, and the cottage is built of granite with small windows, and slate roof, keeping it beautifully cool on hot days, though can be chilly when the sun goes down. The wood and part grey slate floors are perfect for cooling the dogs after their adventures.

We walked back to the cottage, having found a less strenuous exit from the beach than last night! We saw wildflowers, bluebells, red and white campions, wild garlic to name a few. A tremendous diversity of colour everywhere you look from the azure and turquoise of the sea to the bluebells, campions and other hedgerow flowers. There are allotments and polytunnels between the beach and the school, the polytunnels are, I think, making or processing, Island Sea Salt. Plants grow here that I could only dream of growing in my garden at home, such is the microclimate on the Isles of Scilly.

By the time we arrived back at the cottage, both Rosy and I along with two dogs were feeling quite tired and ready for a quiet evening. A small fire in the grate, a warming soup inside us and a good book to read. Bliss.

Rosy's partner had attended a glass fusing workshop on St Mary's today and had enjoyed his day, having hitched a ride on the school boat, taking children over to their secondary school on St Mary's. The children board with friends and families on St Mary's for the week, returning to their home islands on Friday when school finishes. He had been involved in some of these classes before, along with Rosy and they have made some impressive sculptures and ornaments. I am looking forward to seeing this recent sculpture of a wave. The perfect place for inspiration.

Day 3

Another fabulous day, blue sky with few clouds, warmth from the sun, a cacophony of bird-song, no other sound to spoil this peaceful moment. Bertie and I go off for a walk on our own, Misty and Rosy appear to have left already. We head off down the lane towards Higher Town, the lane being the main thoroughfare across the island. I met one person on my way to the beach, they were just off to attend chapel. Bertie met a spaniel who then returned to his master's voice and hopped on the quad bike to continue their chores. At Par beach the tide is low, the sand is white, sprinkled with glitter from the feldspar, mica or quartz in the granite. Bertie's coat is shiny ebony as he darts across the sand to the sea of blues and turquoise. He chases the ball, has a swim and brings the ball back for more.

On the shoreline there is seaweed surrounded by bleached shells and coloured pebbles. I sit down on the sand whilst Bertie explores the dunes. He potters about, sniffing, cocking his head to hear the gulls and other birds above him, running up and disappearing for a few minutes before flying back down the dunes onto the beach to see if I have moved. When he has enough of exploring, he brings his ball back to me and I throw it again for him. He swims in order to fetch the ball which is good for exercise and joints. His coat looks beautiful, not only shiny from the sea water, it is now peppered with silver sprinkles from the sand. A dog with natural bling, now that is different, if only my camera could capture that!

As we walk off the beach by Higher Town Quay, we see a group of people preparing to go snorkelling with the seals, someone else repairing a kayak. At the top of the hill, we sit and rest for a few minutes, it is steep and whilst my health has improved no end, I do still get quite breathless. The bench where I am sitting is dedicated to a local lady, who presumably loved this view. We continue walking and come around towards the granite cottages. A lady asks us to stop, putting her fingers to her lips. There is a fellow with a long-lensed camera and food has been spread on the ground. A rare visitor has been spotted, an American Laughing Gull. It is sitting on the roof of one of the cottages, perhaps eyeing up the sparrows and the food. It has a black beak, slightly more pointed than the common gull, and black tail feathers. The all clear is given and Bertie and I go on our way. It is quite usual to see groups of bird watchers on the Scillies, as there are often rare birds visiting for short spells, before flying to their destinations all over the world. The gull flies on to the roof where the lady lives, she wondered if it had hitched a ride to the islands on a ship, perhaps the cruise ship.

Bertie and I continue up the gentler slope towards North Farm cottage and I muse on the beautiful beaches in Cornwall where Bertie and I walk at home, though rarely having the beach entirely to ourselves as we quite often do here. On our return we sit in the garden, Bertie lying in the sun still glistening from the sea and silver bling, me relaxing in this beautiful garden, sheltered with palm trees, mounds of blue agapanthus, a beautiful old gnarled apple tree, where the thrush is sitting singing out right next to the bench where I am within touching distance. There are camellias of different colours and amongst all of this are a host of wildflowers. Daisies cover the lawn and the sound of birds, with the occasional sound of the small plane bringing visitors overhead and onwards to St Mary's, complete this tranquil atmosphere. The thrush has moved to sit on the arm of the bench and a fledgling perched on the grass behind me. Rosy and Misty are soaking up the atmosphere with us.

A couple of hours later and we are off again. We all walk down to the Seven Stones Inn, near Lower Town, the other end of the island. We took the back lane so that the dogs could have a good run for most of the way. Passing by Turfy Hill, Fisherman's Graves, considered to be a burial ground for early shipwreck victims. We cut through Middle Town down through the trees to the Inn. Yes, with plenty of energy Bertie, and Misty, both built for stamina are enjoying their run. So much to look at on the way with Turfy Hill Point, Wine Cove, there are prehistoric field systems here, identified in places from the ridges crossing over the footpaths. Great Bay is also on our right, also Little Bay and we can see across to White Island, joined to the mainland by a causeway, not safe to cross when the tide is incoming due to the strong currents. White Island is cared for by the Isles of Scilly wildlife trust on behalf of the Duchy of Cornwall and is both a scientific site of interest and geological conservation site, only a short distance ahead of where we turn down through the woods to the Inn.

The sea is stunning, an array of blues and greens and flat calm from our perspective, though when looking closer; there were big waves crashing over the rocks, the white, in stark contrast to the blue. The gorse in full bloom, giving that wonderful coconut aroma, as you walk past. Watching the sea reminds me that these waters hold so much history beneath the waves.

Several people were walking the island today, perhaps they have come over on one of the boats from St Mary's. You soon get to know who is living or staying on St Martin's as you will have probably shared a boat coming over from St Mary's. It is quite a walk from Lower Town Quay drop off point, across the island to Higher Town Quay. Depending on tides you will arrive one end of the island and may be collected at the other, so it is important to make sure that you give yourself enough time to enjoy the delights of St Martin's on the way. I remember Mary and me having to quicken our step considerably in order to catch the boat when we did a day visit back in 2005. We had got rather caught up with the gig teams singing in the pub! There were people there that we both knew.

It took us nearly an hour to walk down to the Inn and lunch was a welcome delight. The crab ciabatta roll was wonderful, tasting so fresh, probably today's catch. We followed fresh local crab with local ice cream made on St Agnes where we visited last year. So many island industries here, flowers, vegetables, farming, salt making, tourism, artists, the island cobbler, ice cream from Troytown Farm and of course fishing. Self-sufficiency is the name of the game if you want to live on a small island. One of the latest industries on the island is sea salt SC Salt which is collected from the beautiful waters of Par beach and evaporated over eight to twelve weeks depending on the weather. I think this is what I have seen when walking back from Lawrence's Bay. A great enterprise, using the beautiful clear waters and making the most of the microclimate here on the islands. It pays to be innovative.

Having enjoyed our lunch, given the dogs their treats and water, we decided on a more leisurely walk back. Walking back down to the road we walked through a cushioned ground of pine needles, we collected firewood. We could see Tresco and St Mary's with sail boats bobbing up and down and the Scillonian ready to take her passengers back to Penzance later that afternoon. We took our time and stopped to look at the wonderful views at various benches and even Bertie sat down a few times to rest, though both he and Misty enjoyed a mooch about whilst we enjoyed the sun. It was a very warm afternoon despite an eastern chill in some areas, particularly when the cotton wool clouds obscured the sun for a few moments. The hedgerows are so colourful with an abundance of flora, gipsywort, hemlock, water dropwort, royal ferns, wall pennywort, yarrow, campions, buttercups and violets and of course hogweed. Beware of the latter, the sap burns skin, blistering, painful, leaving nasty scars as I know to my cost.

When we return to the cottage it is time to relax in the garden and enjoy the sun, the arum lilies and Bermuda buttercups. Rosy has a wonderful memory for the names of wildflowers as well as cultivated and I enjoy being able to put names to these beautiful colours that lurk in the stone walls, hedgerows and this lovely cottage garden. We have had our exercise for the day, the dogs agree and lie flat out on the grass in the shade. Later they will have their late-night garden adventure, just before bedtime, now though they seem to be as exhausted as we are, a rarity!

The fire this evening adds a wonderful glow to the sitting room as we read our books and chat before retiring for a good sleep, to revive our energy levels for tomorrow.

Day 4

Having completed a few indoor chores, Bertie and I set off once again for Lawrence's Bay. On our last visit when we were poking around in the water as the tide came in at Old Quay I found a brain coral, I don't think I had ever seen one before. Today though the tide was very low, making it easy to access St Martins Flats by way of, Cruther's Hill near Old Quay. Tomorrow, Rosy, her partner and I are going to get down and collect seaweed to have with our tea. It should only be harvested and eaten when cut from the source, not when it is floating around. I had not intended walking around to the Flats today, though Bertie clearly thought it was an excellent idea. A new place to explore. Thankfully there was a light breeze rather than strong winds today, meaning Bertie could hear when I whistled for him, not that he always chose to come back! Amazingly, today, he came back straight away and even more surprisingly, still had his ball in his mouth.

As usual Bertie, chewed at seaweed and dug holes in the sand, pretending to hide his ball and then find it under the sand. He did not swim today as the tide was too far away, and too far for me to walk, given we had already walked a long way to get here. I have never seen the tide as low as this; it created a whole new landscape. We met a few people on our route and stopped to pass the time of day. Bertie sometimes tries to muscle in on the conversation, however he had far too many smells to follow, and digging to do! No one was in a rush, not holiday makers like us, nor locals.

Most activities on St Martin's are controlled by the tides, boats coming in and out, bringing in supplies and visitors. The farmers of course are busy, though seem happy to chat for a few minutes before going on their way. The general pace of life is relaxed and leisurely here.

Security is also relaxed, cottages left unlocked, the church as well, so everywhere feels welcoming. The lady doing the flowers this morning said that they have a population of about one hundred people on St Martin's. I imagine the population doubles during the summer and yet it never seems busy. There is plenty of room for everyone. There are of course times, such as gig week and the folk festival amongst other events that bring hordes of people to the islands. There are cottages, an hotel and camping fields on St Martin's. The added population means the island boats are kept busy, and space can be limited, though it has never seemed over-crowded on the islands. I rarely meet more than half a dozen people when Bertie and I are out walking and beach combing. Admittedly I have never been to the islands in the height of the summer, though we were here at Easter in 2017 and noticed a difference in the temporary population boom. The folk festival was also happening, bringing more people to the island. In the evening, occasionally we could hear music and singing, carried across the island by the wind which was rather atmospheric.

I am beginning to recognise the landmarks now, the church tower from the beach this morning, I heard the children playing outside in the school yard as we walked back up the hill to the cottage. Having arrived back and made sure that both Bertie and I had a drink; I sat in the garden making some notes and then read my book. Bertie sat by my feet for about two hours, clearly it was not only me who was tired. We had taken a long walk, much further than I had planned!

This afternoon we took a walk around the block. We headed out towards the Daymark, then took a left turn along the cliff path. We had a good walk and then cut through nearer the top of the hill and back through the village. Last year we went for a similar walk and found ourselves going around the edge of a field with a bull, it had been fenced off with electric fencing. Given I have a pacemaker and need to stay well away from electric fences, it was a bit worrying, even more so as I had Bertie on a lead on this very narrow area, not even a path really. I think Rosy and I held our breadth all the way around and were thankful to get back onto the main path! I am all out of hill climbs this afternoon, it has been a wonderful day of walking and now I feel I have done enough. Bertie agrees!

The island is small and if you walk to the highest point, you should always be able to find your way back, assuming a thick blanket of sea mist has not descended upon you! This adds to the feeling of safety and relaxation. Even I am unlikely to get lost! The road, is the only direct thoroughfare across the island, so you will always find your way home. Knowing this, makes it more fun to explore.

The beautiful hedgerows and dry-stone walls were particularly noticeable on our walk today. Stones of all shapes and sizes balanced on top of each other. Sunlight shining through the cracks, at a distance looking like the finest filigree silver, from the granite rocks and stones, sunlight on mica as it is in the sand that glitters beneath your feet.

I searched and found some beautiful shells and stones on the beach this morning, all different shapes and sizes, turned by the sea and bleached by the sun. I have loved stones and shells all my life and tend to always have my head down when walking on a beach.

What a lovely quiet and relaxing day it had been, just what holidays are all about. Clean air, relaxation, exercise and a beautiful landscape to free your mind, and recharge.

Day 5

This morning we walked again where the dogs could run, towards the Daymark. I also popped in to see the island shoemaker. The handmade shoes just look so beautifully comfortable and colourful. I am quite tempted.

Later in the day, after a little relaxation we took the dogs for their second walk, they are getting a little too used to a two walks a day system, not sure how we will manage when we get home, though last year Bertie, quickly got used to his home routine again. Once again, we walked up the back lane where the dogs have their freedom to roam, run, sniff and explore. It was misty, with sun sneaking through clouds shooting straight rays to the ground every now and again, making the weather changeable, when the sun came through bringing unexpected heat.

We headed down to the Inn for lunch and sat outside in full sunshine whilst we ate. The view from the Inn was stunning, the shining spangled sea, the black rocks, along with the trees and flowers surrounding the Inn's boundary walls including palm trees. A real sun trap of tropical plants, white sands in the distance and bright blue seas. Very exotic.

After lunch we walked down towards Lower Town Beach where the dogs had another run, before we boarded the 'Voyager', one of the inter-island boats, owned by Mary's cousin. We were heading out to see the Eastern Isles. There were not many people and plenty of room to move about. We watched the seals and birds, as the boat slowed alongside the various small islands. We were lucky enough to see an auklet on the water, oyster catchers, shags / cormorants, black-backed gulls, a fulmer, related to the albatross I am told, along with gannets and guillemots as well as several grey seals, both in and out of the water. Quite an array of wildlife on and around these Isles. Rosy and her partner are good at recognising and naming birds.

The mist continued to wrap itself around the islands, cloaking the boat and giving us sneak views as it lifted briefly and moved around with the sea breeze, temporarily obscuring some of the Isles and then, slowly bringing them back into view with a mystic veil surrounding them. As we sailed around the Isle of Nornour, our attention was drawn to the Iron Age settlement, a number of Bronze Age huts have been uncovered which showed extended use, and was likely used through to the Roman times. Fine gold jewellery and roman coins had been found there. The settlement had a round house, storerooms and an open-air courtyard, so the boatman told us. Little was visible now of course. The finds are now safely housed in the museum on St Mary's. In 1862, the Steamship Earl of Arran hit Irishman's Ledge and went down just off Nornour Brow. When Ian and I visited the little church and church yard at Old Quay on St Mary's we saw the memorial for the Earl of Aran, amongst many others, for lost sailors drowned after their ships were wrecked on these treacherous isles. There are six uninhabited islands that form the Eastern Isles. Having seen them shrouded in heavy mist today it was easy to see how so many wrecks occurred over the years.

Bertie seemed nervous today, he kept shaking and pushing up close to me, sitting on my feet as he does sometimes when he does not understand what is happening. Perhaps he was reliving our rather rough crossing from Penzance only five days ago.

We enjoyed our boat ride around the Isles despite the inclement weather, having left the boat behind we walked back along the beach, scattered with shells, sea glass and pebbles, the tide higher, the dunes rising to our left, stabilised with marram grass. Only a few people on the beach, just one couple near Lower Town Quay. A wilderness, a paradise of striking islands. It had been a warm, though muggy day, enclosing the beauty of this island in curtains of mist and fog throughout the day.

Walking along the cliffs first thing this morning, hearing the fog horn was atmospheric and I wondered what it would feel like hearing that sound when you were out at sea in a boat; hopefully reassuring, though perhaps somewhat eerie as well. These islands have been notorious for shipwrecks over the years. Captains and sailors did not have the safety equipment, sonar and other gadgets that are now standard issue.

The end of another wonderful day, so much to see, to learn and to experience on these beautiful islands, steeped in history, tradition and mystery.

Day 6

Wind howling through the rafters this morning and throughout the night. A force 7 gale apparently, it was forecast for yesterday, though crept up on us overnight and was playing havoc with the roof slates on our little cottage, rattling and banging as the wind lifts and wraps itself around them in a tight hold. Rosy and I took the dogs for a run up towards the Daymark, their usual morning outing. As we came around the corner a gust of wind almost knocked us off our feet. We continued to walk up the back road for shelter, bent double against the wind as we struggled to progress. It was relentless, definitely not a day to walk on the cliff paths. The dogs took no notice and enjoyed their freedom to run and sniff, off their leads. I just needed to be able to keep up! We walked out onto the moor, still throwing the ball for the dogs when they asked to chase it. We had to be mindful of the wind direction, and with our backs to the wind made sure that the ball stayed on the path rather than becoming lost in the moorland bracken and heather.

Looking across to the islands, the waves crashed down on the blackened rocks, white spray flying high above them. Once again so different to the other side of the island which was blue sea lapping gently against the rocks, blues, turquoise and that hint of purple that we see so often. Hardly any spray, and no big waves visible. So different from glimpsing the calm sea yesterday through a veil of sea mist.

The gorse did not give off the same aroma today, perhaps it is the heat of the sun that releases its scent. The campions and bluebells are being blown, bent double and yet have the strength not to break, their colours vibrant against the grey of the day, perhaps it is that beautiful clear air over the islands that makes everything look so bright.

Before we walked back, I made my way to the top of the hill, bowing to the wind, I could almost see the entire coastline of the island around us. On such a small island, only two miles by half a mile, it was surprising how different each part of the coast was; particularly as regards the colour of the sea, the current, and general ebb and flow. It is like looking down on separate worlds.

Rosy had booked to go and view a cottage today; it was on the market! We took the dogs back to North Farm and walked the short distance to view the property. It was built in beautiful traditional granite with a slate roof, in 1832 and was a listed building. We learned a great deal from the present owner about what it was like for her, living her life on St Martin's. The domestic water over the whole island is from bore holes, and reliant on getting enough rainfall during the year. Supplies are shipped over from the mainland and of course if the weather is too bad, or the sea too rough, you just have to wait until the boat comes in! The best route to survival, is to become very much a part of the community and as self-sufficient as possible. This cottage had an orchard and the tell-tale signs of having once had a large vegetable garden. The lady had many stories to tell and was interesting, having a wealth of first-hand knowledge, information and experience of life on the island for twenty-four years; she and her husband had brought up their family there.

Close to the cottage was the Methodist Chapel, which last year hosted a wonderful exhibition of photographs through the years. The photographs included Royal visits, local industry, family life, the lifeboats through the ages and all things related to living on the Isles of Scilly. A fascinating portrait of island life.

After sitting down to a delicious cream tea, just a few yards up from the cottage, we set off again; collected the dogs and walked down to Lawrence's Bay where once again the dogs enjoyed the sea, running, chasing the ball and swimming. Bertie managed to bury his ball so deep that he actually lost it altogether. The holes he dug in the sand looked as though turtles had been nesting to lay their eggs.

We stayed on the beach for a couple of hours watching the birds swooping and diving along the sand-dunes. There was a cruise ship about to depart St Mary's and we saw the Scillonian leave to take its passengers back to Penzance. Just one more day on this lovely island and we will be heading home ourselves. I think Rosy may have been daydreaming about a life on St Martin's having visited the cottage this morning. I could see her living there, and naturally I would be a frequent visitor. I got the impression that Rosy's partner whilst he likes visiting the island, is not thinking of making the leap to a permanent move. We all need dreams and this is hers.

The air ambulance circled overhead and landed somewhere near Lower Town Quay, before taking off again about forty minutes later. It would head back to Cornwall, probably to Royal Cornwall Hospital Treliske in Truro. We had seen the coastguard leave Higher Town earlier, along with some volunteers. No doubt we will hear later what had occurred. Clearly everything was under control and the people or individuals involved were being taken care of, and are hopefully safe and well.

On our return to the cottage, we sat in the garden for a while. The dogs dried off and then shook some of the sand out of their coats. We went inside, lit the fire, and sat down to supper. Another wonderful day, full of surprises, fresh air and exercise. The day began with a gale and ended with calm and warmth from the sun. A fire in the evening warmed the cottage, hearts and souls. Perfect.

Day 7

This morning I made a quick trip to the one and only island food shop. I bought ice creams made from the creamy milk produced by the Jersey cows on St Agnes, at the Troytown farm, a couple of books for Freddie, my youngest grandson and then I took Bertie for his first walk of the day around the block. I visited the island cobbler again as I have looked at his beautiful handmade shoes so often, I thought I might treat myself this time. I tried on a pair in my size and they just fitted like a glove. I picked out a dark purple leather and when I get home, hope to put in an order. Rosy and I are off to visit South Africa next year and they would be so comfortable for the trip. By trying on a pair, I can now confirm size, design and have my colour swatches handy. I can't wait.

Having returned to the cottage and left Bertie there with Misty and Rosy's partner; Rosy and I went off to view a second property. The views were stunning from every angle looking out over the islands, the sparkling sea adding mystique all around. The plot was huge, a beautiful mature garden surrounded the property, which in addition had a serviceable vegetable garden to the side. The garden would take a great deal of maintenance, though, with the views, and the rather tropical weather here, that would not be a hardship. Rosy and I have always been interested in properties and over the years have renovated a few, helping each other out. As we get older, we are less inclined to renovate, perhaps just decorate.

The owner of the property was not an islander and it was interesting to hear from him, what it was like to live on the island for just six months of the year. Living on an island requires you to be an extremely well organised person as we found out from the owner of the first property. Bulk items needed to be ordered from the mainland and then transported from St Mary's out to the smaller islands, this can include your winter fuels, tools, garden compost, as well as your food shop and sundries. The island shop is wonderful for daily bits and pieces and a week's holiday, though catering for six months is a different ball game. The island farmers and gardeners provide wonderful vegetables and soft fruit in season, though winter crops are limited.

As today is our last day we head off to Lawrence's Bay to walk out on St Martin's Flats, as the tides have been extraordinarily low Rosy is keen to pick and cook seaweed. Most seaweeds can be eaten, so long as they are picked from their source. Rosy was interested in identifying different species and then cooking some up for tea. She did not pick very much, just enough to have a taste. We all walked on the flats for a few hours, Rosy searching out seaweeds, her partner and me beach combing, some interesting finds out in areas usually covered by sea. The dogs had a wonderful time exploring pools and smells that were new to them.

Rosy found several species of seaweed which we would sample later, and we traipsed back through the dunes and marram grasses to the road and up the hill back to the cottage.

We collected our coats, as the sun had disappeared behind the clouds, and went off down the hill to Little Arthur's Café. A late and very pleasant lunch of fresh crab rolls for us and tripe treats for the dogs. Well, we all deserve a treat on holiday don't we.

Bertie became very anxious, and panicky at one point when a bee dropped on him from a flower. It reminded me and perhaps him, of his nasty experience last year when we had gone for a walk around the man-made lake at Pencarrow House, he had disturbed a wasp nest, he had been badly stung as the wasps had got into his coat. All I could think of was to get him into the water to drown the wasps, it took days to get them all out of his long silky beautiful black coat. He had been quite traumatised, understandably.

After lunch and a good rest, we set off for another walk which would take us in a circle, and up another steep hill back to the cottage. Once again, we sat in the garden with the dogs at our feet and ate ice cream that I had bought in the morning! Last year we visited the island farm where the ice cream is made, and of course sampled a few flavours. The garden is so sheltered that we could relax in the warmth from the sun with just the sound of the breeze gently rustling through the hedge and the plants surrounding us swaying gently to-and-fro.

Sue Lewington used to live at this cottage, she is a local artist. Sue has been busy working with the school children here on St Martin's for

Art Week. This evening we walked up to the gallery to see the children's work, following their creative and exciting week. There were some clever ideas, demonstrating a keen eye for colour, it was exciting to see the work on display, what a wonderful celebration of their creativity and amazing inspiration from their surroundings.

I had visited the gallery earlier on in the day and the owner asked if I could mind the shop whilst he went to sort something out. One of the things I love about St Martin's, you get to know people and there is a real sense of trust and community. I happily looked after the gallery for half an hour and even sold a couple of items. North Farm Gallery showcases local work, artists display their original work, as well as prints and cards, there are crafts including jewellery, gifts and calendars. Beautiful work, such clever, creative people.

We kept the seaweeds to eat this evening, they were tasty, quite peppery and succulent when fried in olive oil, salad with fennel from the garden and some three-cornered leaks made a much healthier end to our stay than the massive portion of fish and chips that we finished with last year, down at the café near the harbour, delicious as it was.

Tomorrow we must pack, clean up, and leave the cottage before ten o'clock in order to catch our boat over to St Mary's where we will then have a few hours to look around before boarding the Scillonian to sail home. Last time when I was here with Rosy and her daughter in 2017, we nearly missed the boat as we had visited Juliet's Garden for lunch and then walked on around the cliff path. We sat above Carn Morval Point watching the sea and seabirds, the dogs mooching around and then stretching out resting beside us. Rosy decided that she might walk a little further along the path and we suddenly realised what time it was. Looking over to the harbour, it did not seem far, though walking was a different matter. We did however catch the boat! I had not noticed my watch for the whole week as no sense of time had been required.

Leaving day

Up early this morning and all hands-on deck! The cottage needed cleaning top to bottom, no signs of dog hair to be left behind, or sand, cases to pack, including all the dog's paraphilia, beds, bowls and balls. We needed to leave the cottage by 9.30am as the inter-island boat leaves Higher Town Quay at 10.00am and the dogs will need walking first. Our host kindly transports our luggage to the quay for us, so that we are free to walk the dogs down the hill and give them a quick run on the beach before boarding the inter-island boat to go over to St Mary's. Our last walk on St Martin's for this year.

This morning the boat is doing a round island cruise, so we have an hour and a half boat trip. Higher Town to Lower Town, Tresco, St Agnes and back to St Mary's, thank goodness the dogs had a run first. A beautiful day and perfect seas. We motored passed the rocks, that yesterday had been part of the Flats where we had collected seaweeds and shells. Amazing how far out the sea had been, yesterday we stood on the sand and the dogs rushed around and today we sailed over it, through the deep seas with barely the top of the rocks showing above water. The sea was a brilliant blue and though not flat calm, gave us a memorable ride.

Having arrived at St Mary's we loaded our luggage into the container to be winched onto the Scillonian later. We were free then to explore until 15.45 when we would board the ship homeward bound. We took the dogs onto Town Beach and gave them a good run. Bertie was so interested in all the new smells that he wandered off and had to be put back on the lead. Having had a week of complete freedom to roam he needed to get back into the habit of staying close and coming when called. St Martin's is virtually traffic free, whereas St Mary's has larger and more varied traffic as well as an influx of daily visitors. We did some window shopping, thinking about small gifts to take home for the grand-children and then went along the front on Porthcressa beach to the café. We met up with Rosy's partner who had been over to the gallery to collect his fused glass sculpture from the workshop he had attended earlier in the week.

We sat in the beautiful sunshine, overlooking the bay, the dogs sat under the table in the shade whilst we had some lunch. We enjoyed a good salad bowl with avocado, pistachio and beetroot. As the café was busy, we moved down the promenade to a seat where the dogs could sit under the bench, or on the grass behind. Rosy said see you later, to her partner as he was heading off to the airport for his flight from the Isles. He would collect us at Penzance this evening on our return.

We had a perfect view of the sea; the blackened granite rocks the tower at Buzza Hill to our left and sail boats bobbing up and down on the rippling waves. Small colourful boats pottering in and out of the bay and larger yachts further out to sea with their sails up, gibs tight, skimming waves. The sun sparkled on the water like starlets twinkling as the waves lapped against rocks, beach and hulls. The sky was clear blue, not a cloud in sight. We saw what we thought was Rosy's partner's small plane fly over on its way back to Lands End airport and waved him off.

Rosy and I took it in turns to go and do some shopping so that the dogs could enjoy stretching out in the sun prior to their final run on the beach before boarding the ship, as it is a three-hour journey home, from when you find your seats.

This time Bertie enjoyed a proper run and swim on Town Beach. The boats in the harbour are all shapes, sizes and colours bobbing gently on the waves, they are held on their moorings from the beach. Lines of rope stretched almost the full length of the beach and we could see the lifeboat station at the far end towards Porth Mellon where I had stayed on my second visit to the Isles of Scilly with my old friend Mary.

Mary had loved the islands and visited at every opportunity. These isles have a way of rekindling memories as if they were only yesterday and I could not help but think about my previous visits and the people with whom I had enjoyed the different islands and experiences.

After the dogs had enjoyed a good run on the beach, paddled, and had a freshwater drink, we walked back to the harbour and were ready to embark, and sail home.

The sun remained hot for most of the journey home, the sea calm and the decks busy, a contrast to our journey out last week. We had managed to find a seat at the top of the gang plank, sheltered and sunny. We met up with our host who was off to the mainland for a few days, and also Sue, the artist who had worked with the school children and the gallery.

What an amazing week we had, perfect weather for dogs and walking. Peace and quiet to think and write, good company. We had spent all week with a mix of doing our own thing, meeting together for meals and quiet evenings by the fire. A perfect blend for a relaxing, enjoyable holiday.

On our voyage home we saw tankers on the skyline, Longships Lighthouse in all its glory, though no high waves crashing above it this evening. As we approached Penzance, the sight of St Michaels Mount is always wonderful and several people were out in their kayaks. youngsters jumping off the pier into the icy, silvery blue water. We are so lucky to live in this amazing county with all of this on our doorstep. The boats in the harbour were swaying and bobbing on the ripples, the light was changing, and the sun appeared to slowly descended into the sea, the sky a mixture of oranges, silver and pinks.

We were collected, as planned from Penzance, and then once we arrived back to Rosy's we let the dogs out in the garden for a run around, whilst we had a quick cup of tea. I packed my car and headed home, about one and a half hours drive. Bertie was very quiet in the boot of the car, on his bed, and perhaps having happy dreams of running along beaches and swimming. When we finally arrived home, he ran around the yard, checking the smells and adding a few fresh ones of his own, just to make sure everyone knew he was back. Bertie was so pleased to see Reggie when we arrived home, his half-brother, they rubbed noses, walked around each other and then went in the house together whilst I unloaded the car. I felt sure that the dogs would communicate all night about their different adventures from the week!

We had enjoyed a wonderful week, plenty of exercise, sunshine, fresh food, good books and above all good company. A wonderful seven days in a most beautiful location. Whilst tired that evening, it was a relaxed and comfortable feeling. I can't wait for my next visit.

I hope that you have enjoyed reading about the Isles of Scilly and our holiday. It is one of the most beautiful locations you can imagine.

Sadly, due to the pandemic I have not been able to visit the Isles of Scilly since this amazing trip. I hope that I will again before too long. Whilst it is all on my doorstep it may just as well be the Indian Ocean for the climate, plants and white glistening sand!

If you have enjoyed this story, perhaps you would be kind enough to put a review on Amazon or Goodreads or even a mention on We Love Memoirs Face book page. **We Love Memoirs | Facebook** Thank you. You can follow me on Amazon if you wish, see my previous books as well as be the first to hear about new ones coming soon.

White Horses and Sunbeams **https://www.amazon.co.uk/White-Horses-Sunbeams-Cathy-Mayes-ebook/dp/B07S1M3TJ3/ref=sr_1**

Matt and Pandora **https://www.amazon.co.uk/Matt-Pandora-Cathy-Mayes-ebook/dp/B08SJ3KCFT/ref=sr_1**

Out of the Quill Box **https://www.amazon.co.uk/Out-Quill-Box-Secrets-family-ebook/dp/B0916HQMQR/ref=sr_**

Wallace and Me **https://www.amazon.co.uk/Wallace-Me-Did-choose-him-ebook/dp/B0B85KHFWD**

Thank you to Andy Bogen for formatting and preparing the book for publishing and also to Mark Bernstein (Bernstein Cartoons) for the great illustrations.

Thank you to Rosy for being a great friend and travelling companion. And thank you to my son Philip, Lucy and his family for giving me my beautiful Bertie. My constant companion.

Printed in Great Britain
by Amazon